23 photographs.
Light of Night Town

Henry W. Rennengburgton Jr

ISBN-13: 978-1507620168
ISBN-10: 1507620160

DEDICATION

To my true friends

CONTENTS

1 CHAPTER
THE HOLIDAYS IN THE WINTER DAYS

The winter.
Peace light in obscurity of night.
The light it is like the real painting and music of town that author sees and feels in this book.
The light photos addresses to feelings of readers.
Also, dear reader, you can feel and understand world of light in night town.

Once again photos addresses to special feeling of readers.

This book or photo album is
the appropriate place to speak about the brilliance light.
There's the chance of being into the glamorous world of light.
When you watches the photos very much to see something of them;
they will show themselves in all their brilliance.
23 color photos show the beauty of light decoration of town.
Each photo gives the joy each man who takes the beauty, who is able to receive
the beauty who wants to know and to receive the beauty with joy.
Author sees this beauty and gifts this joy to all.

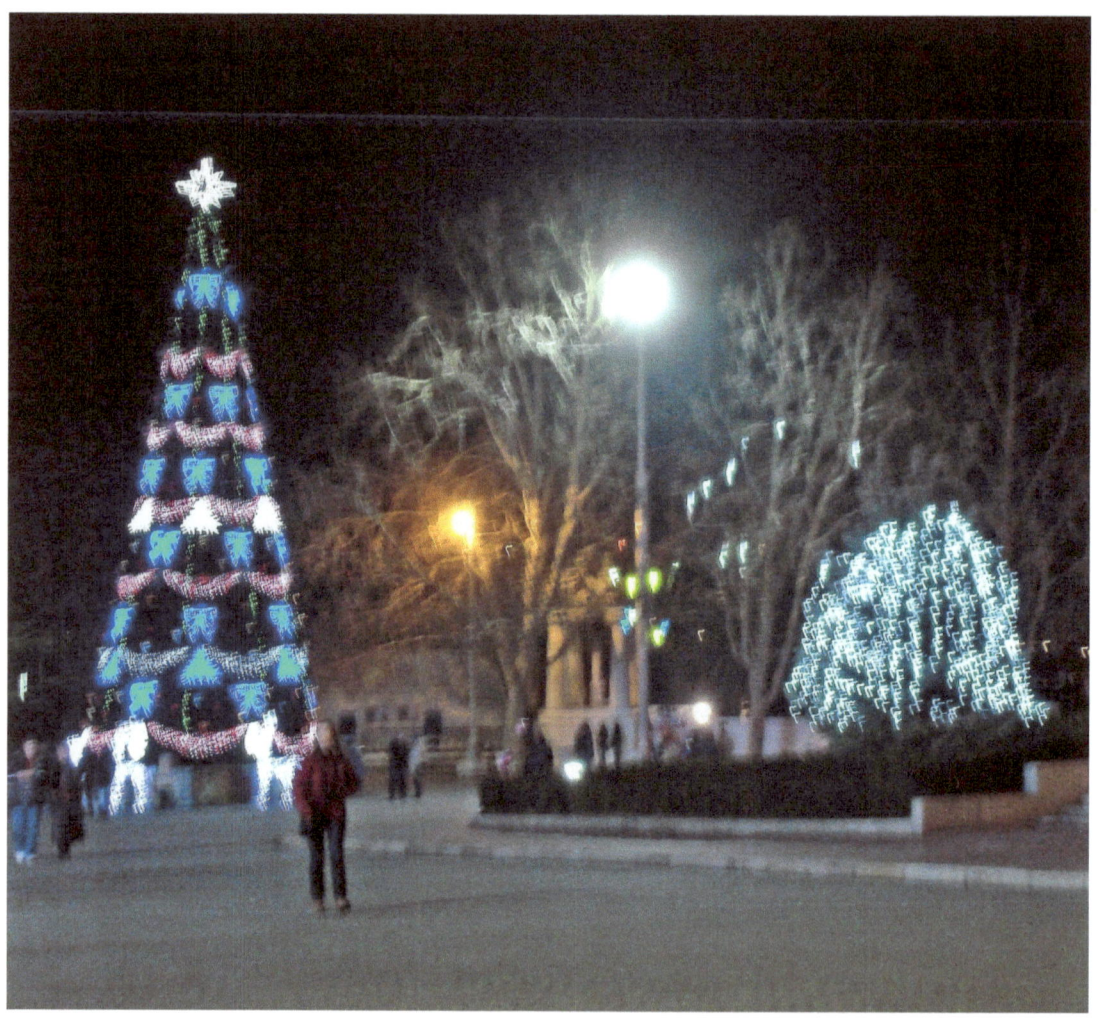

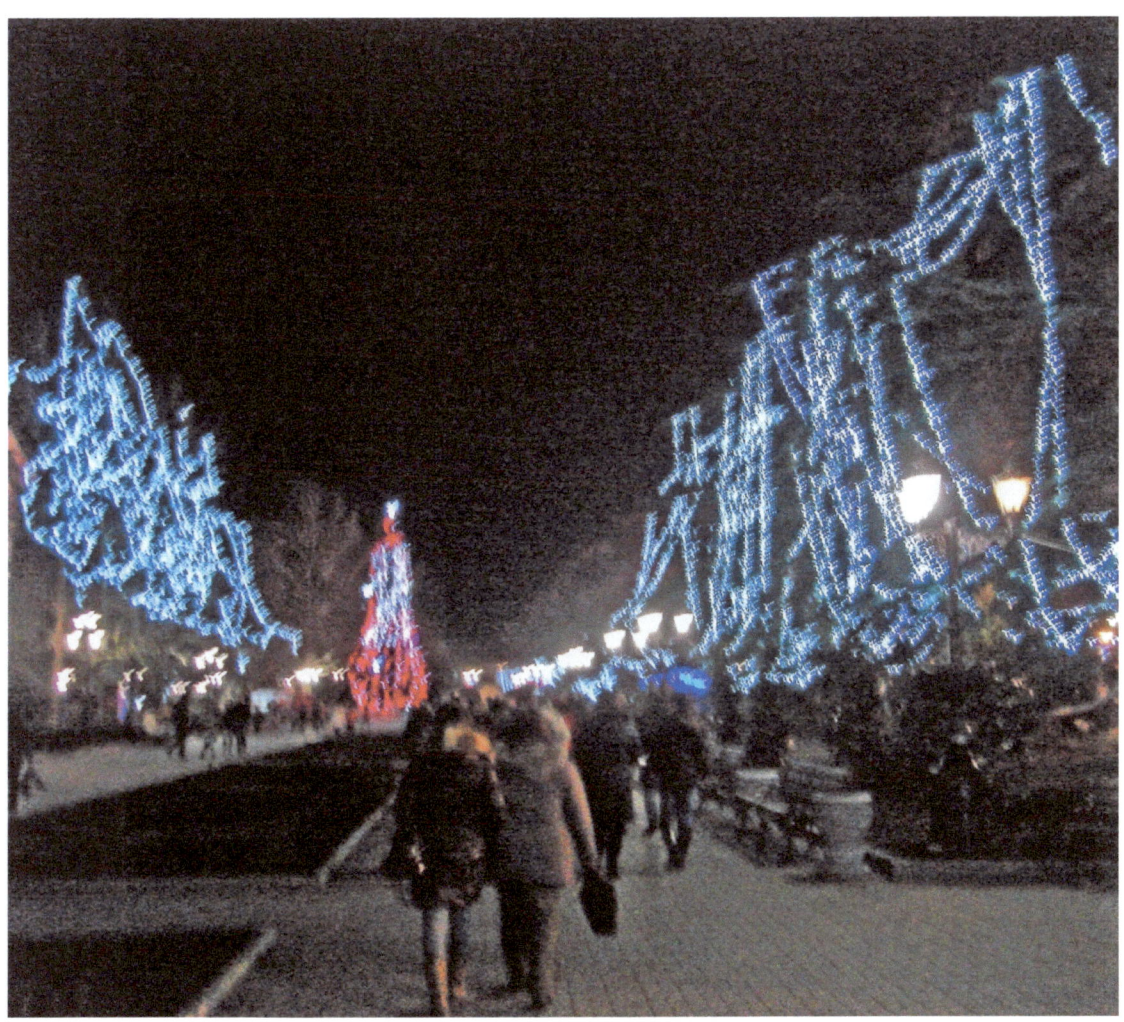

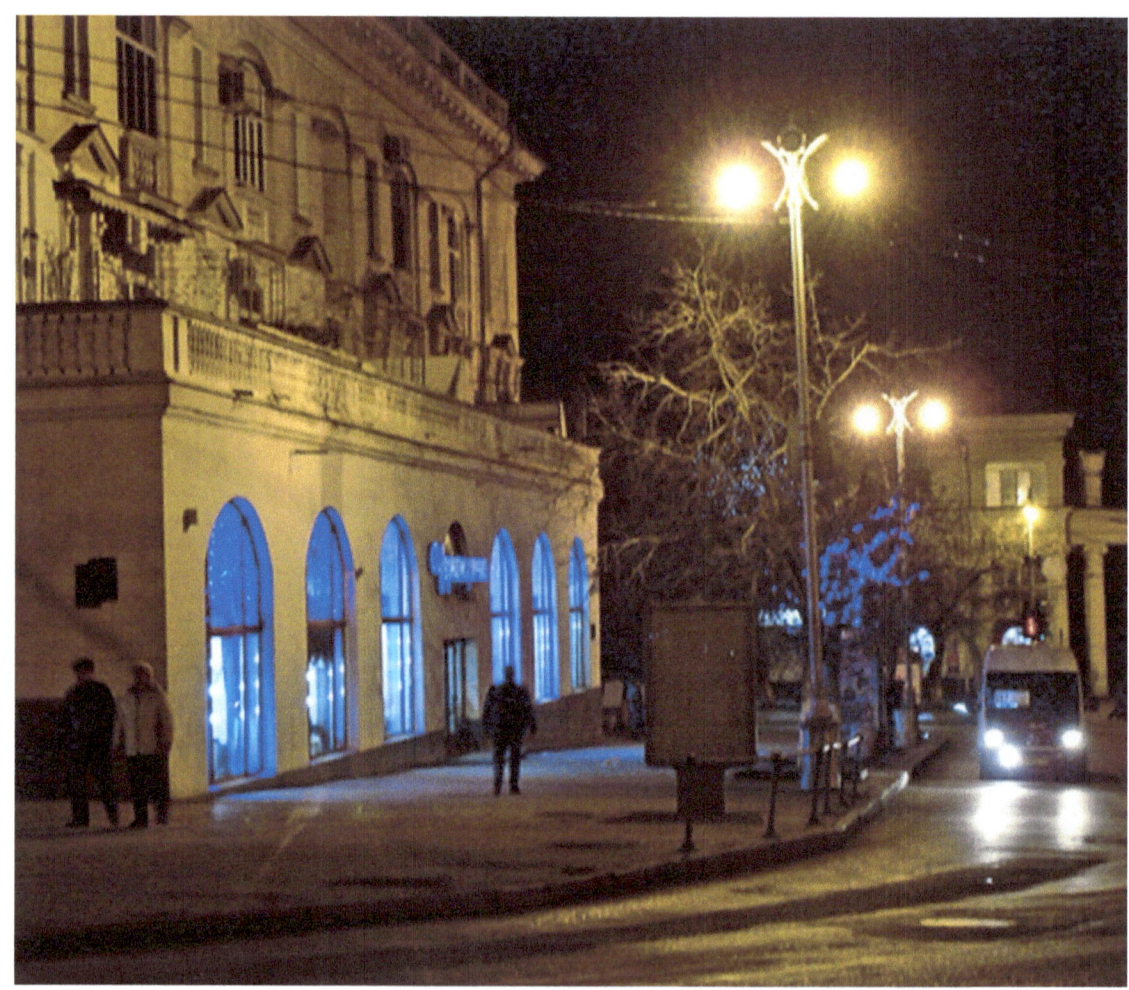

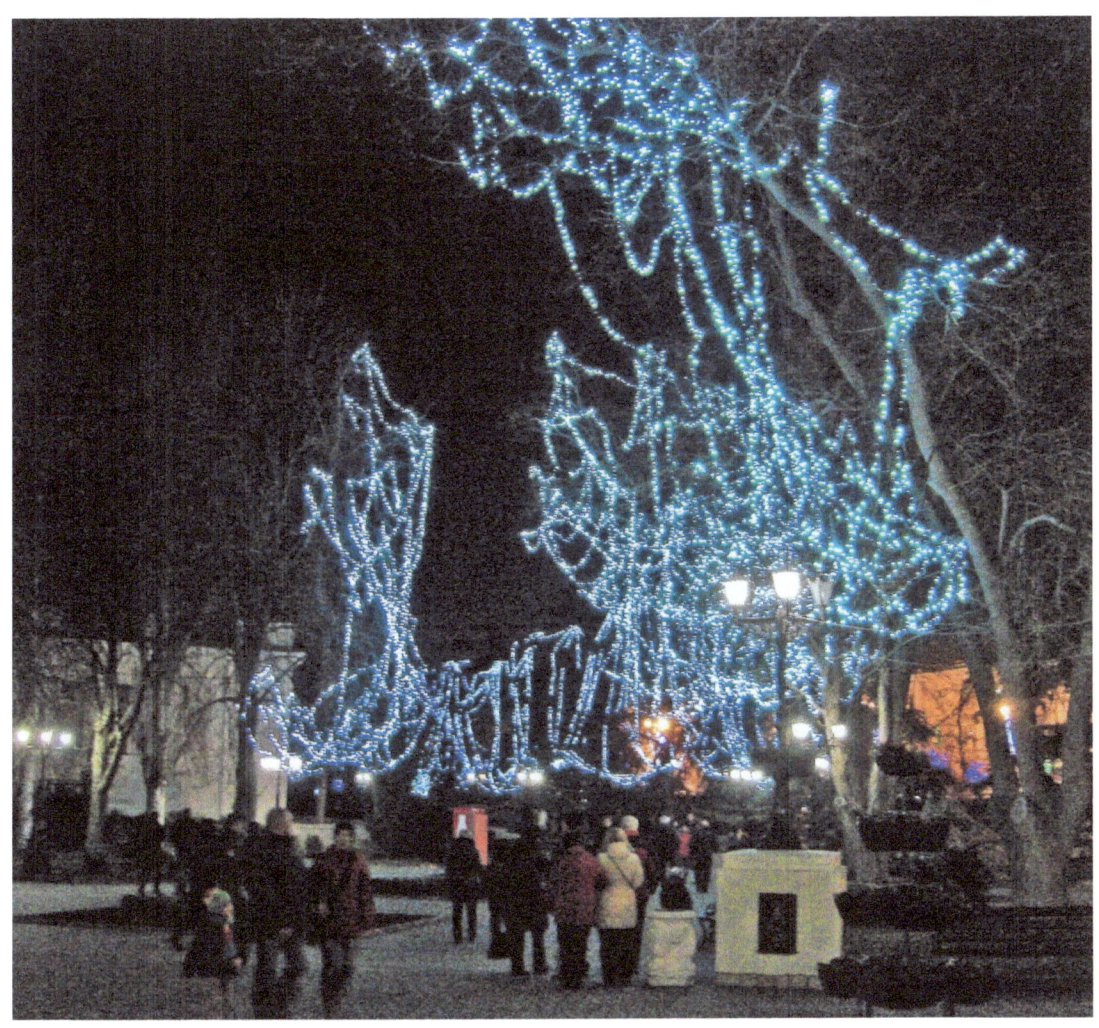

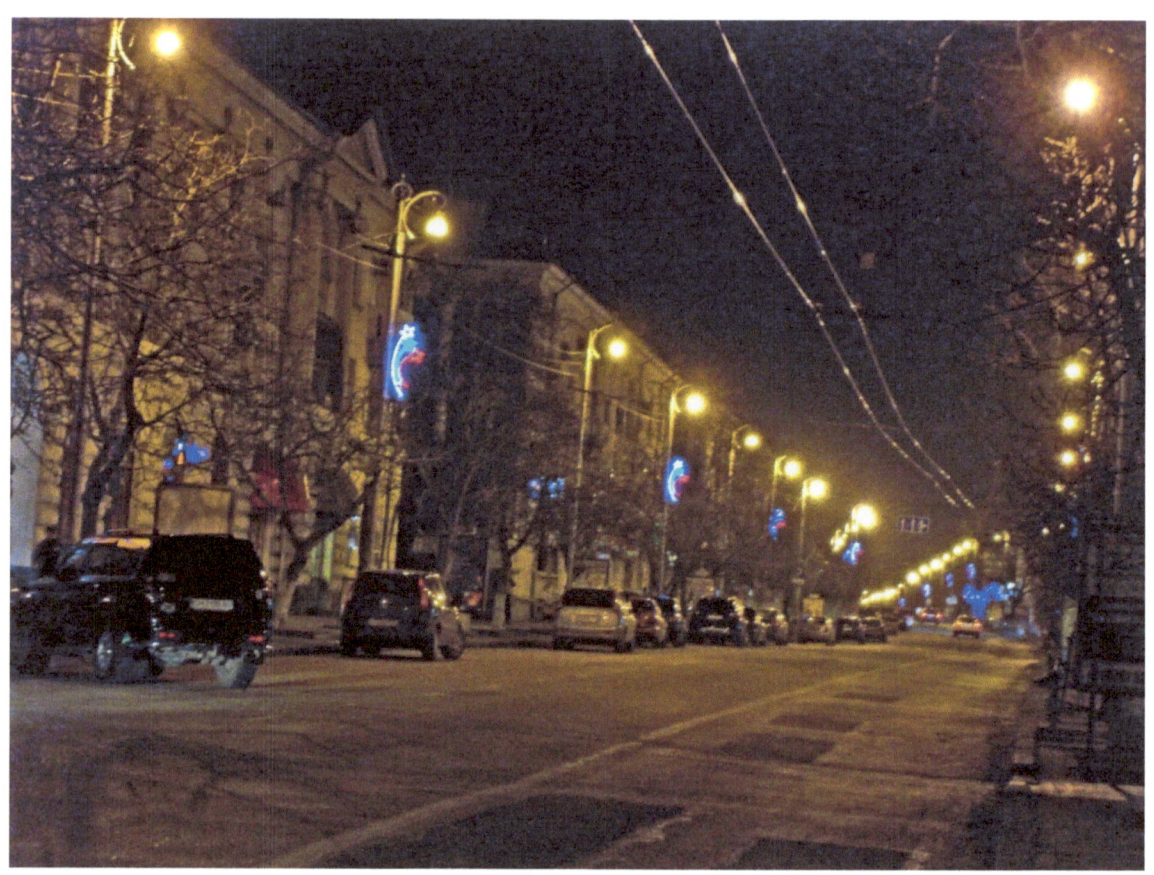

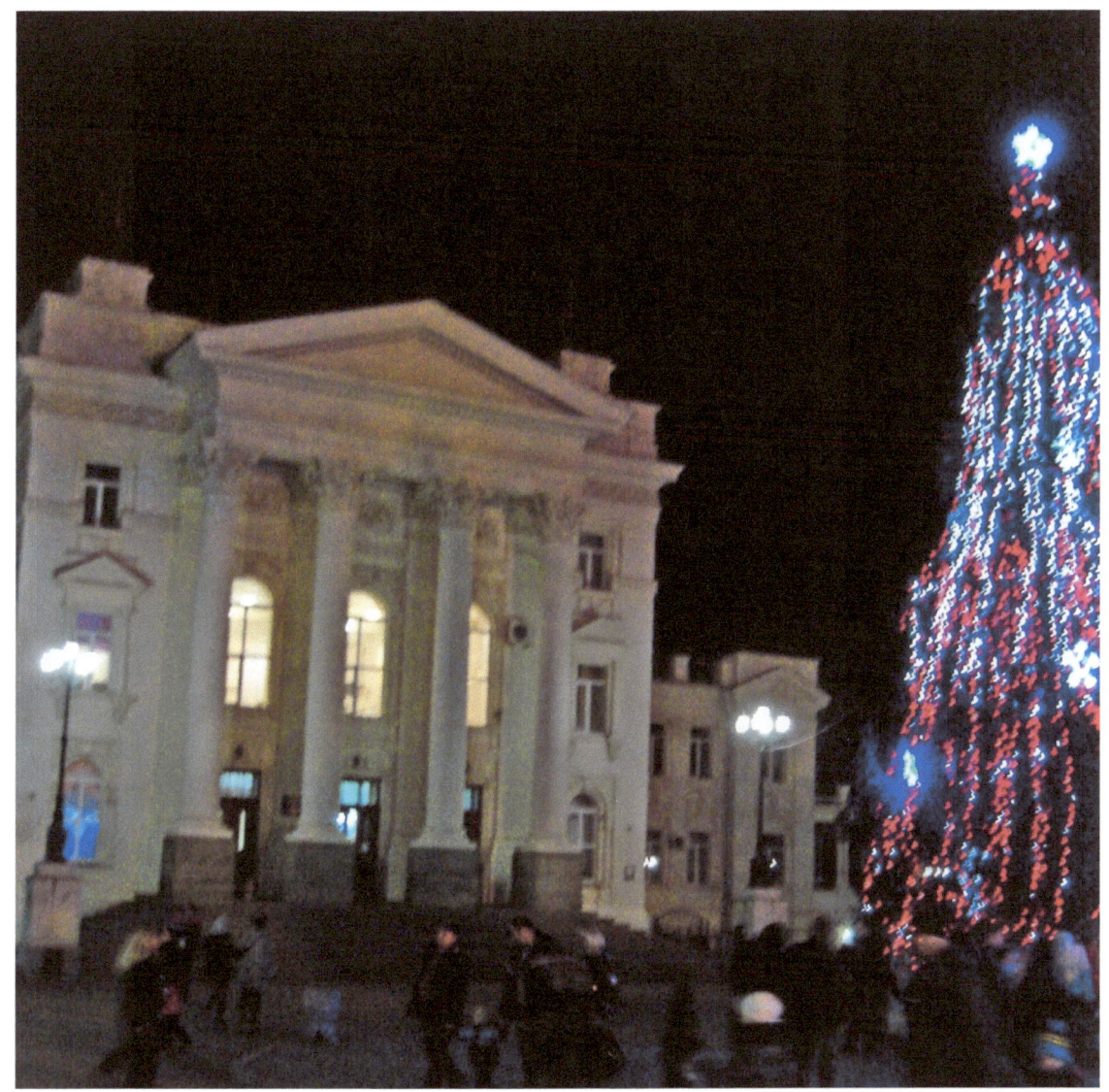

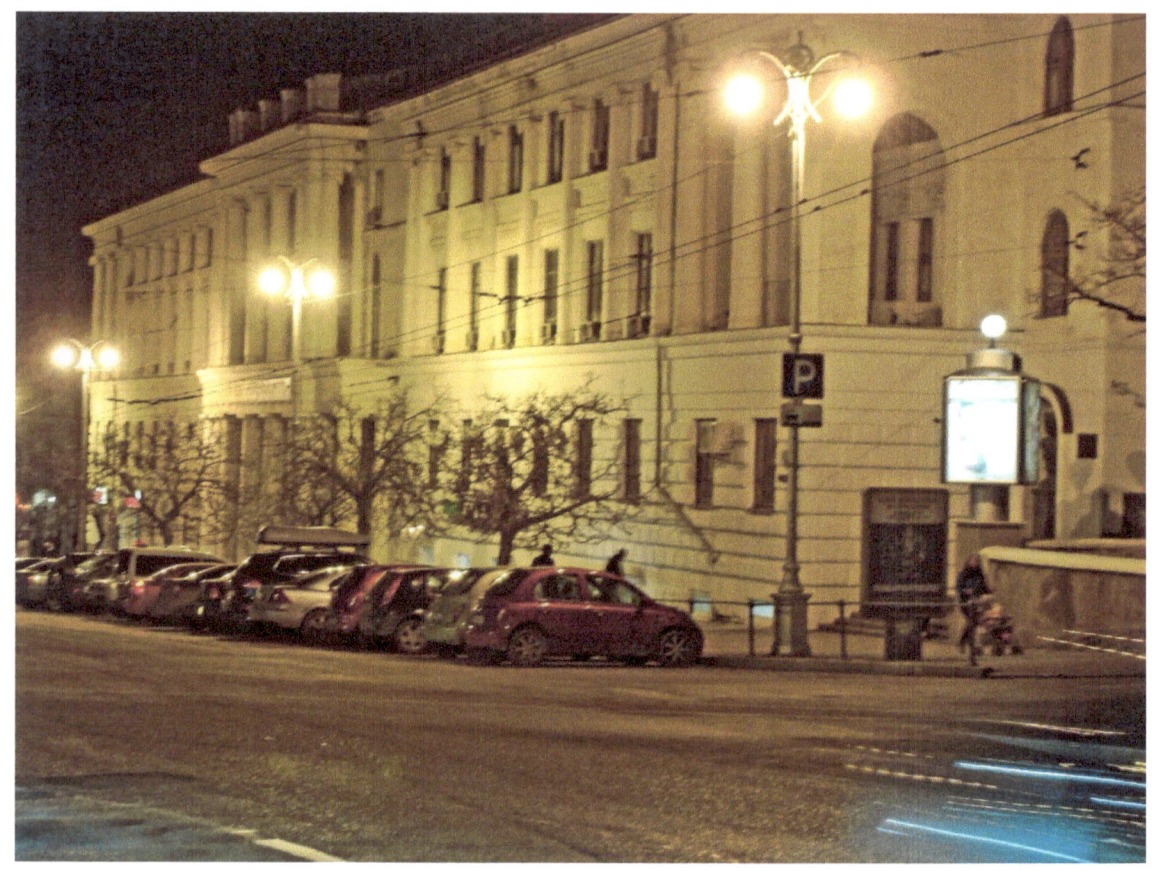

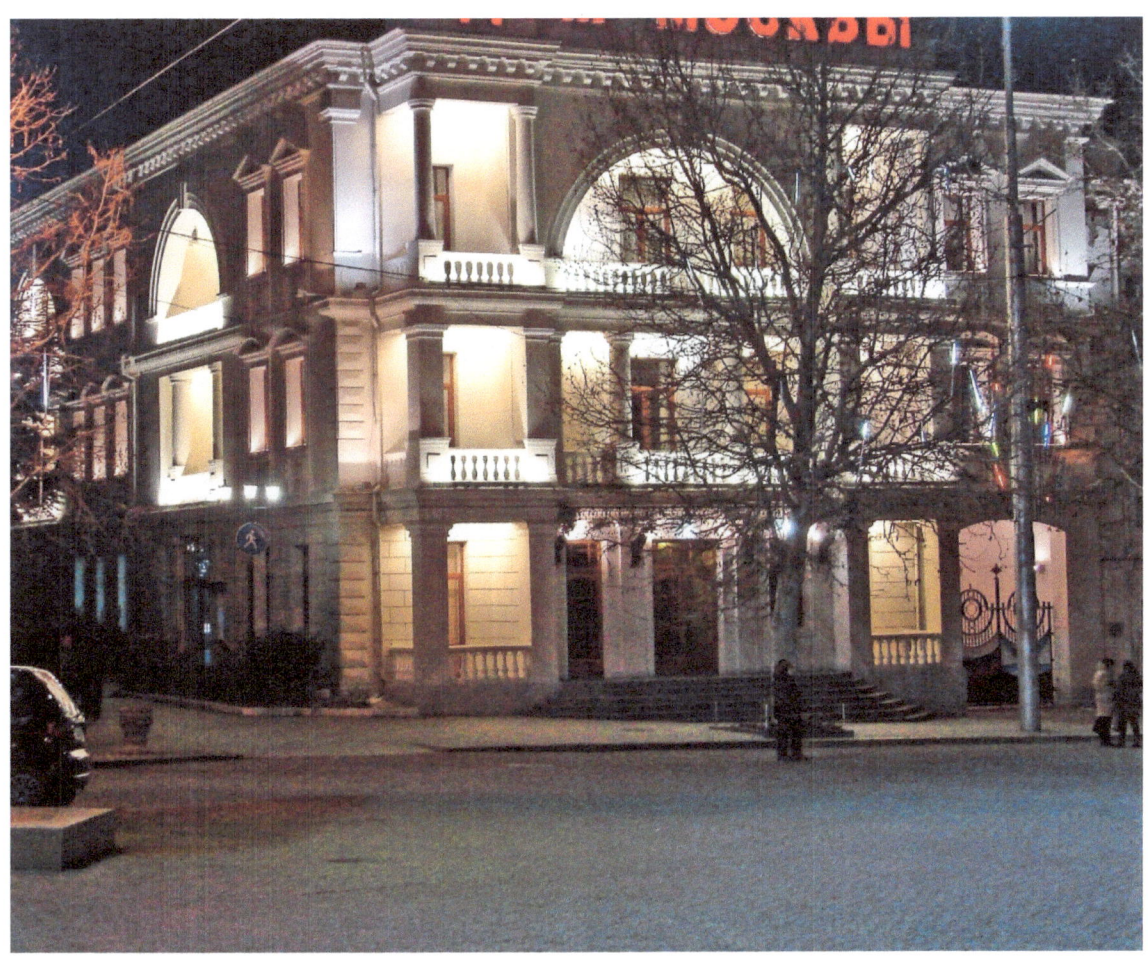

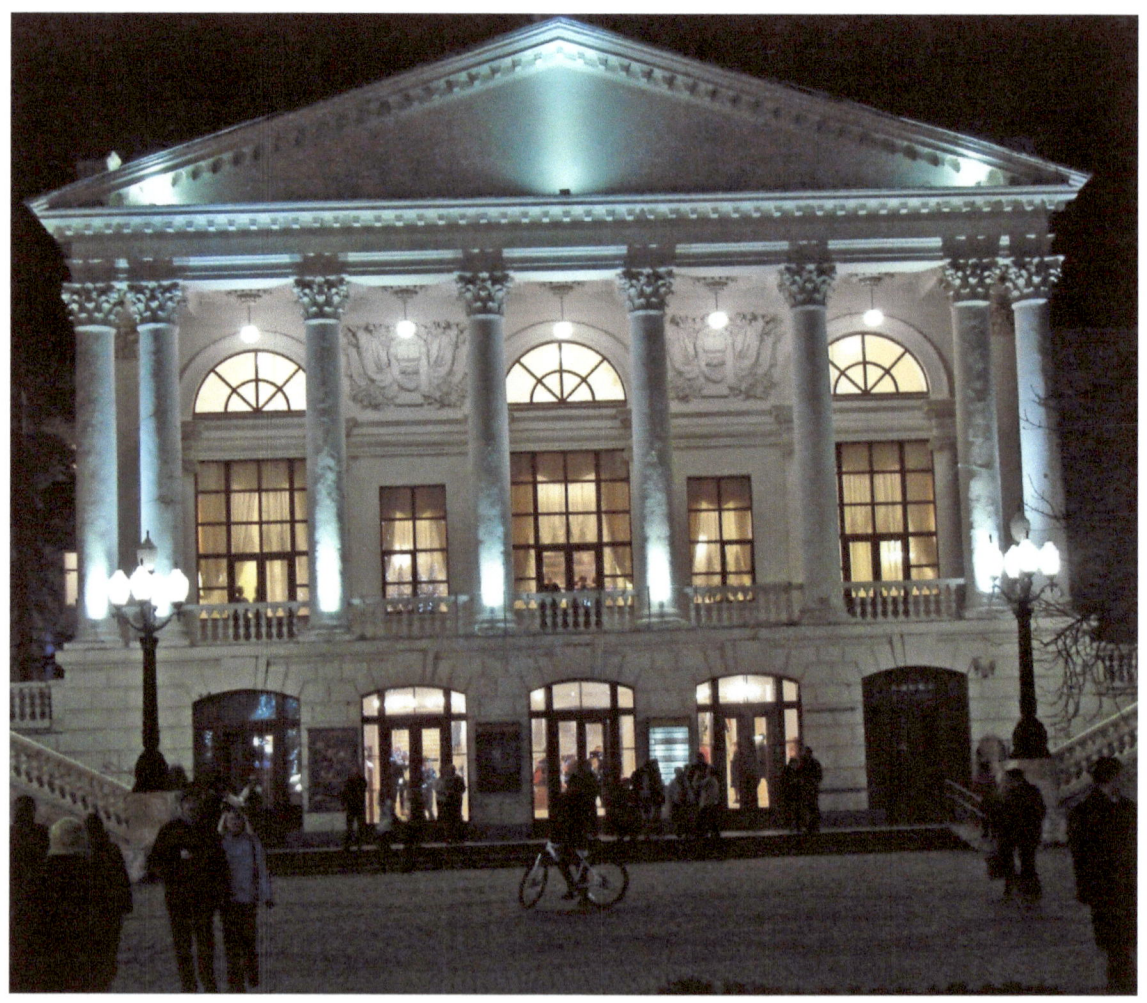

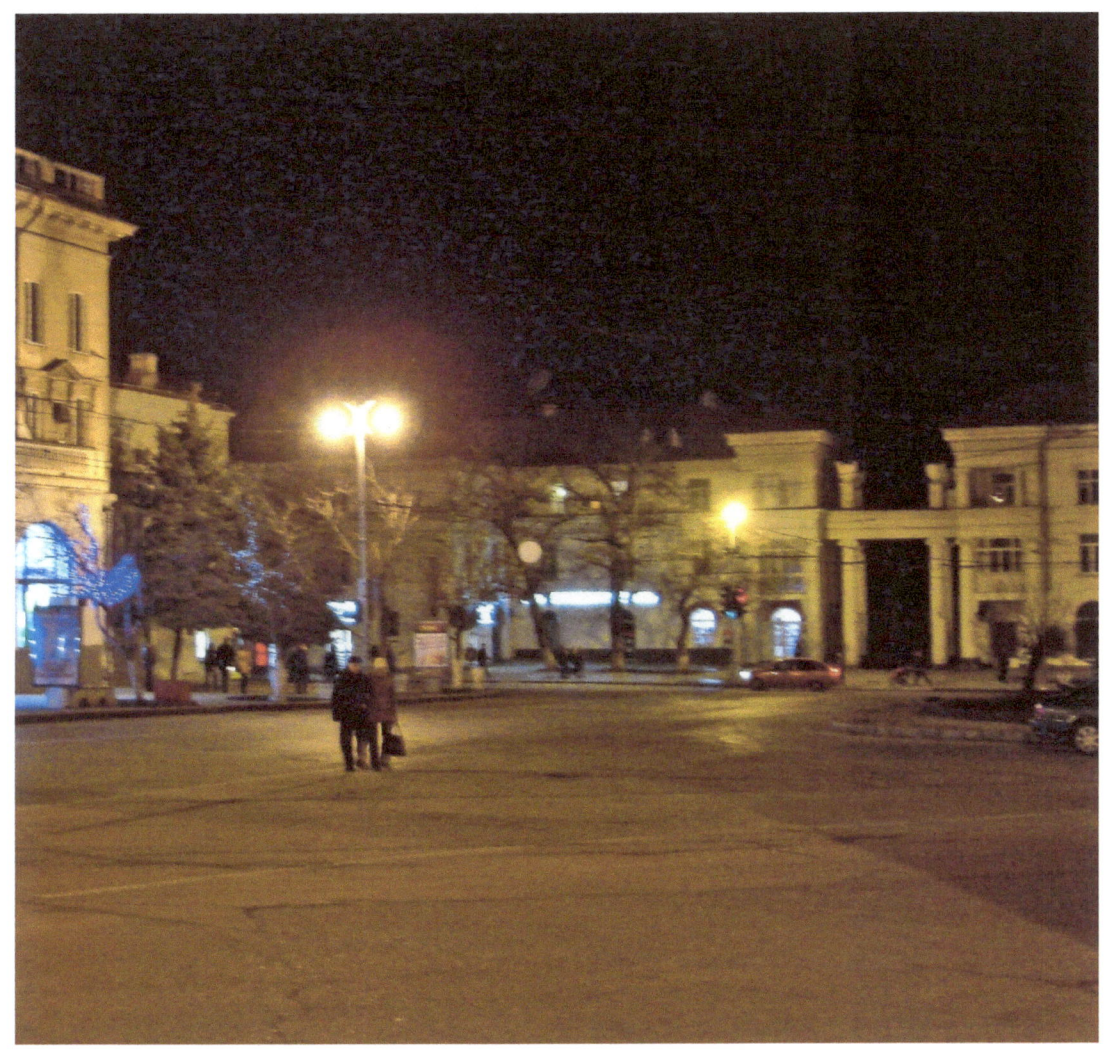

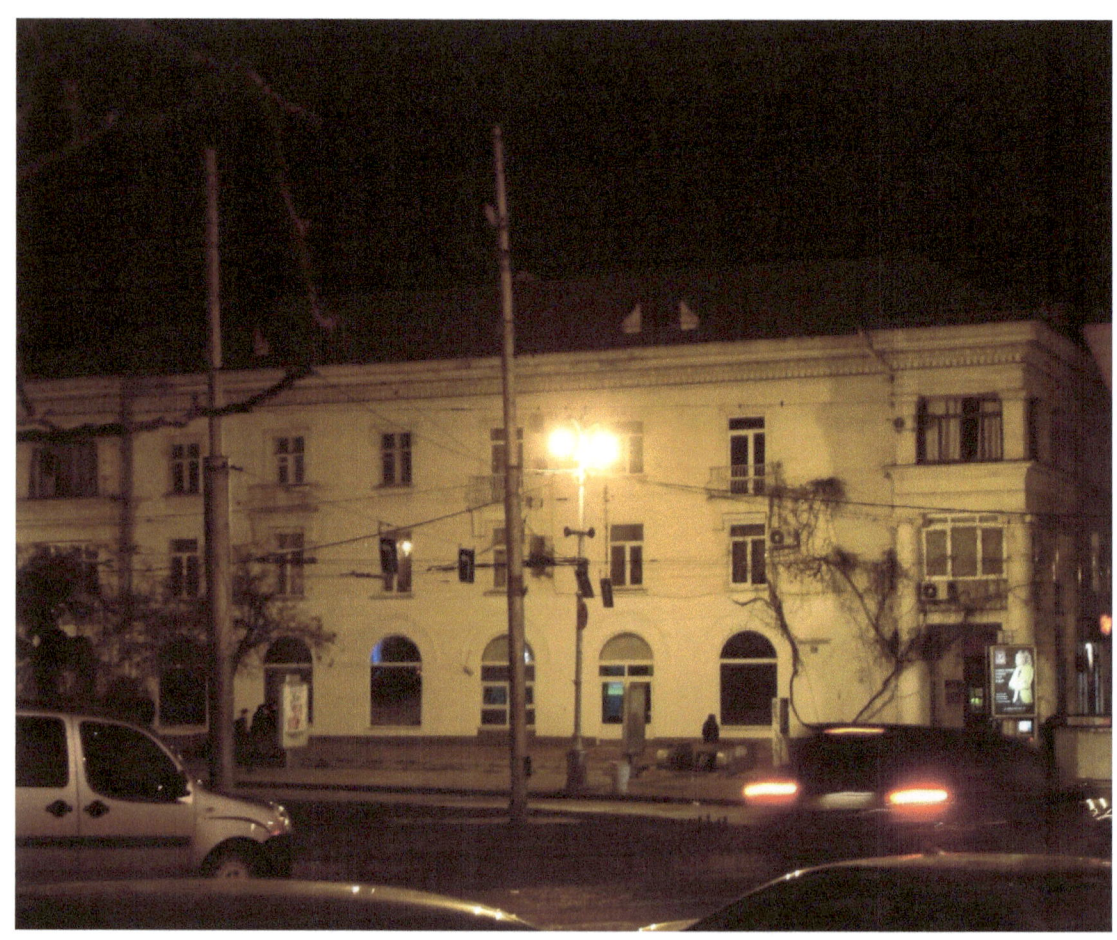

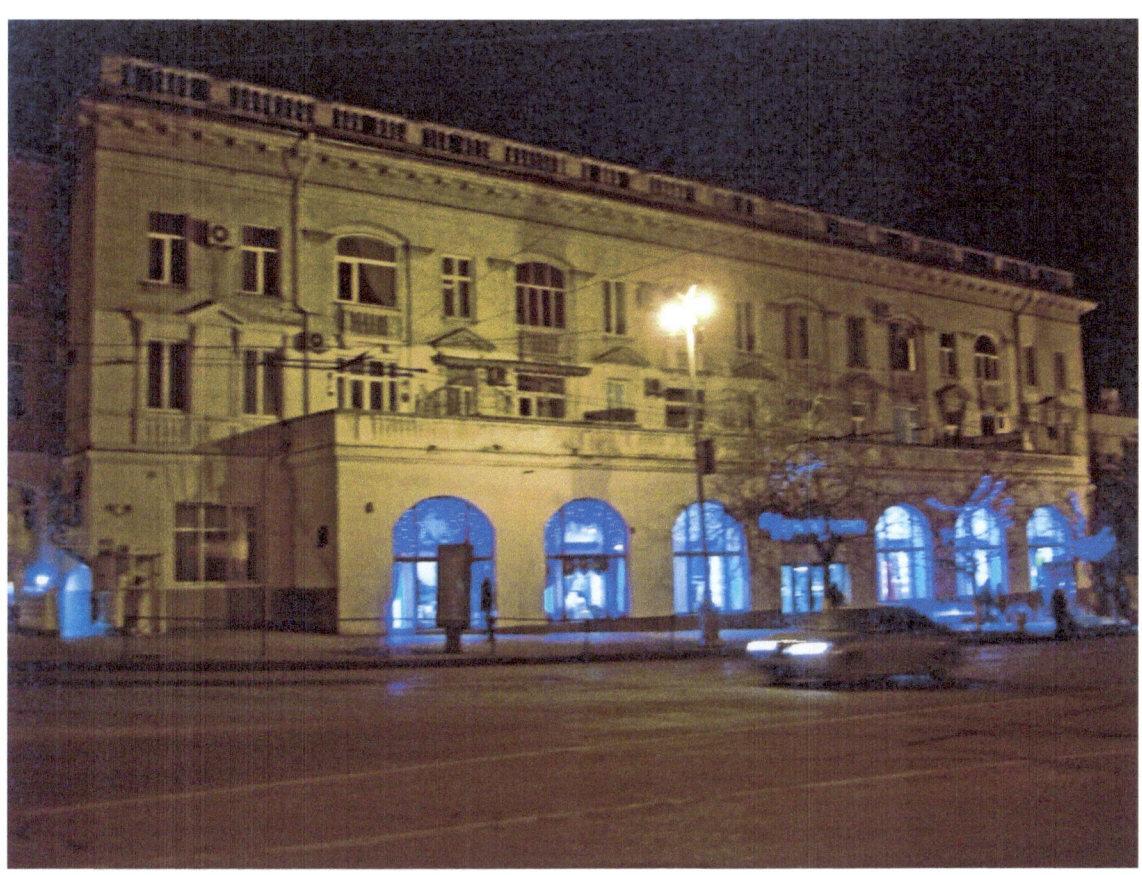

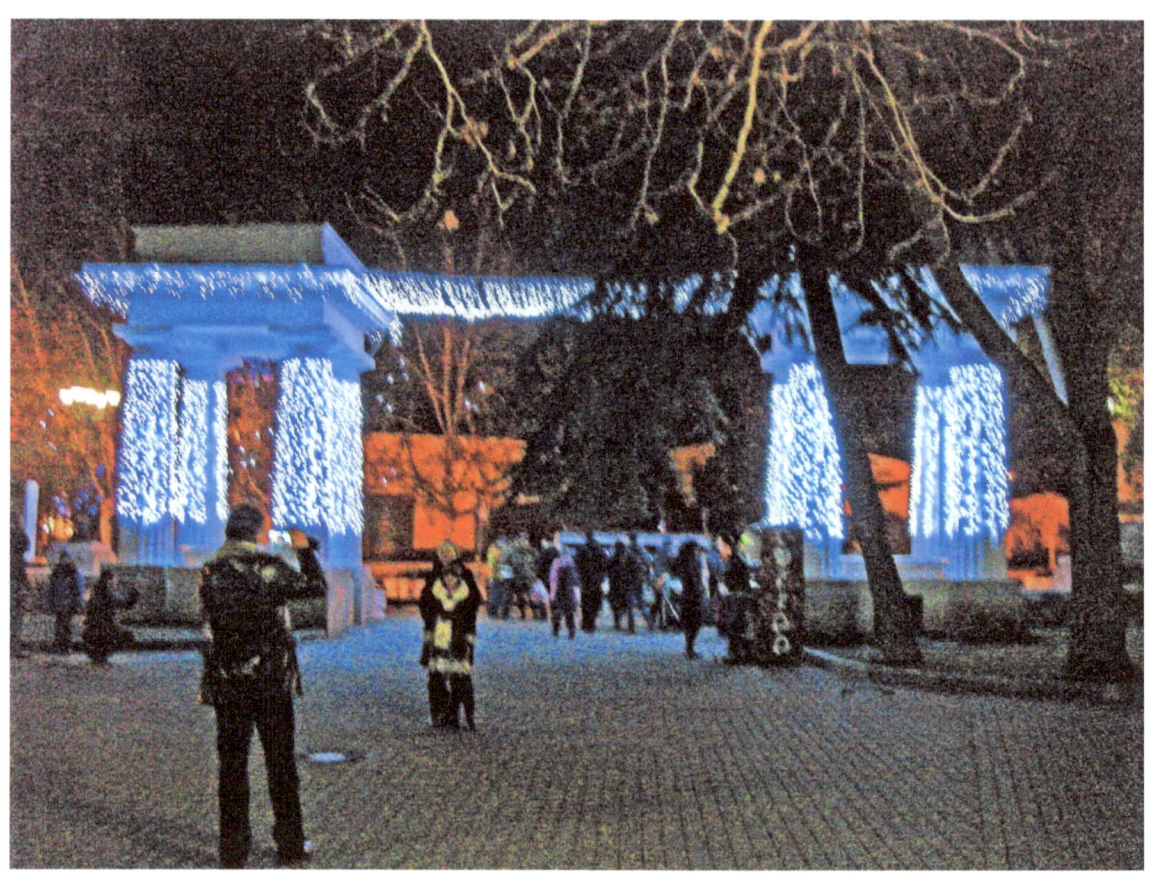

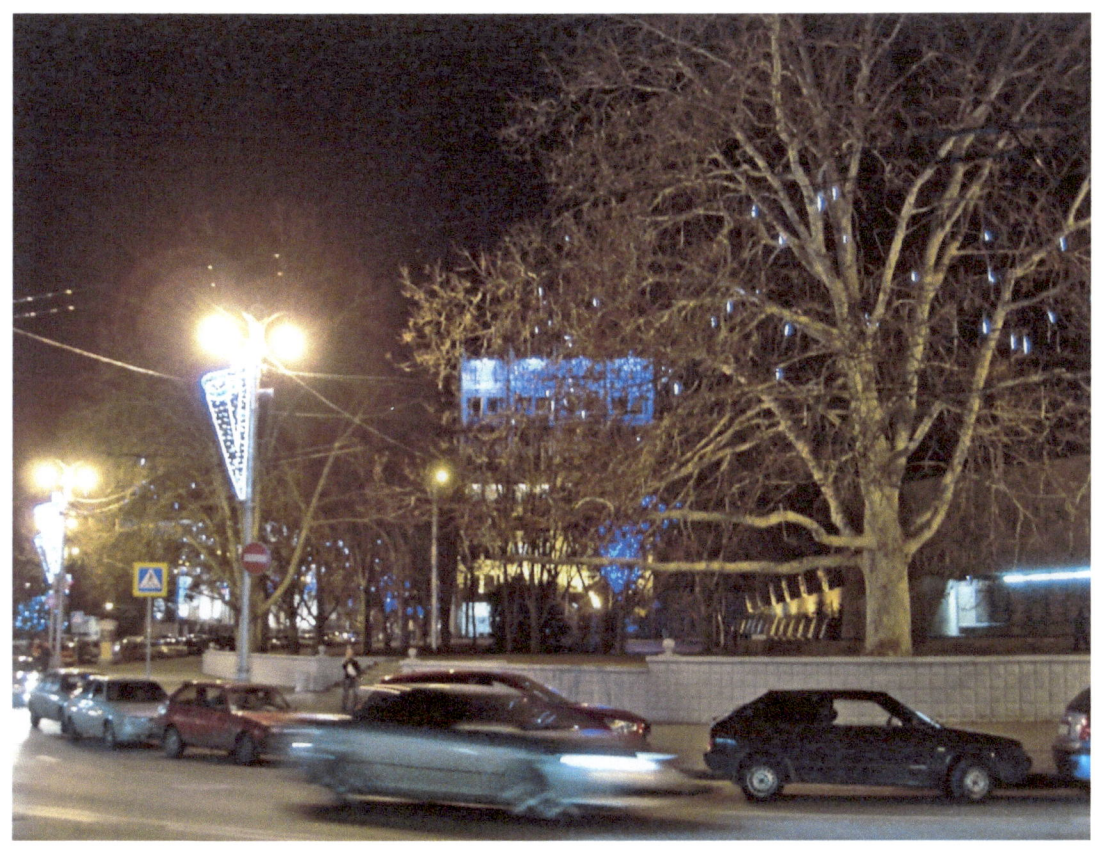

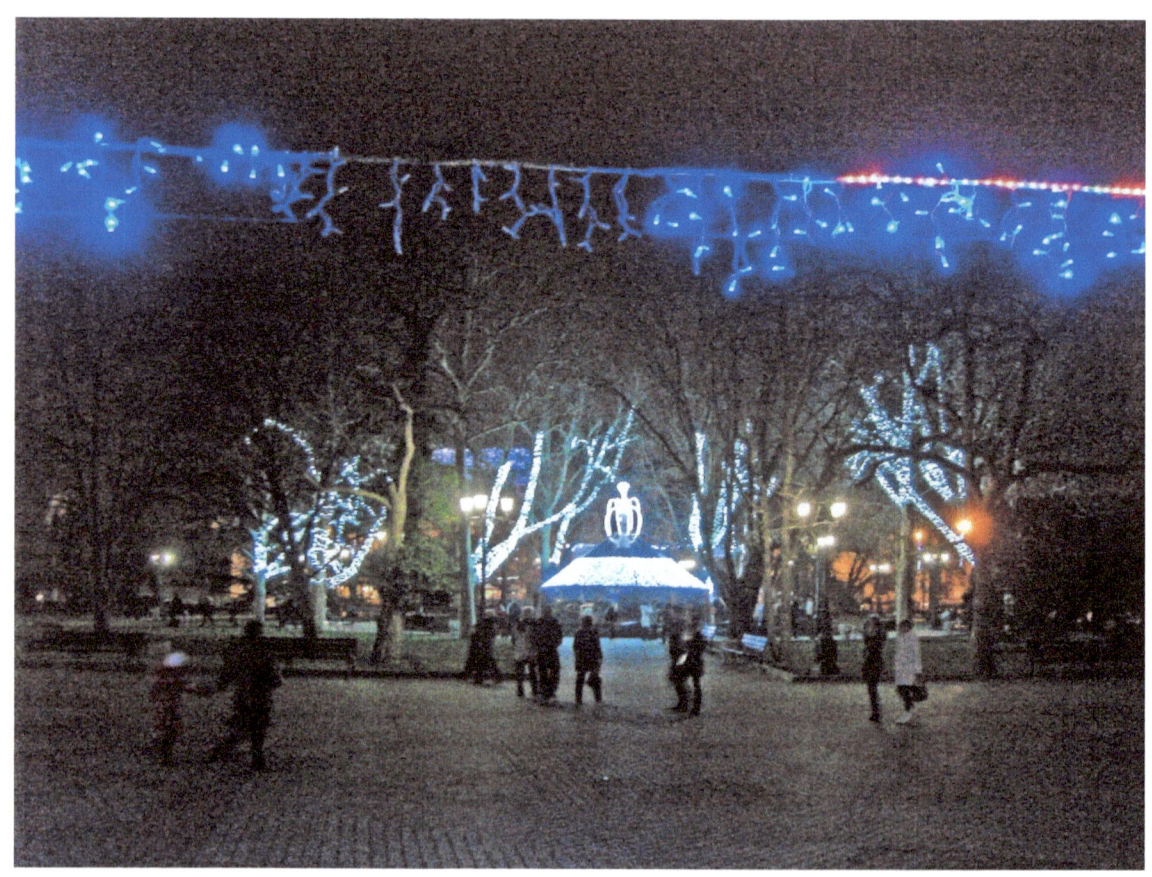

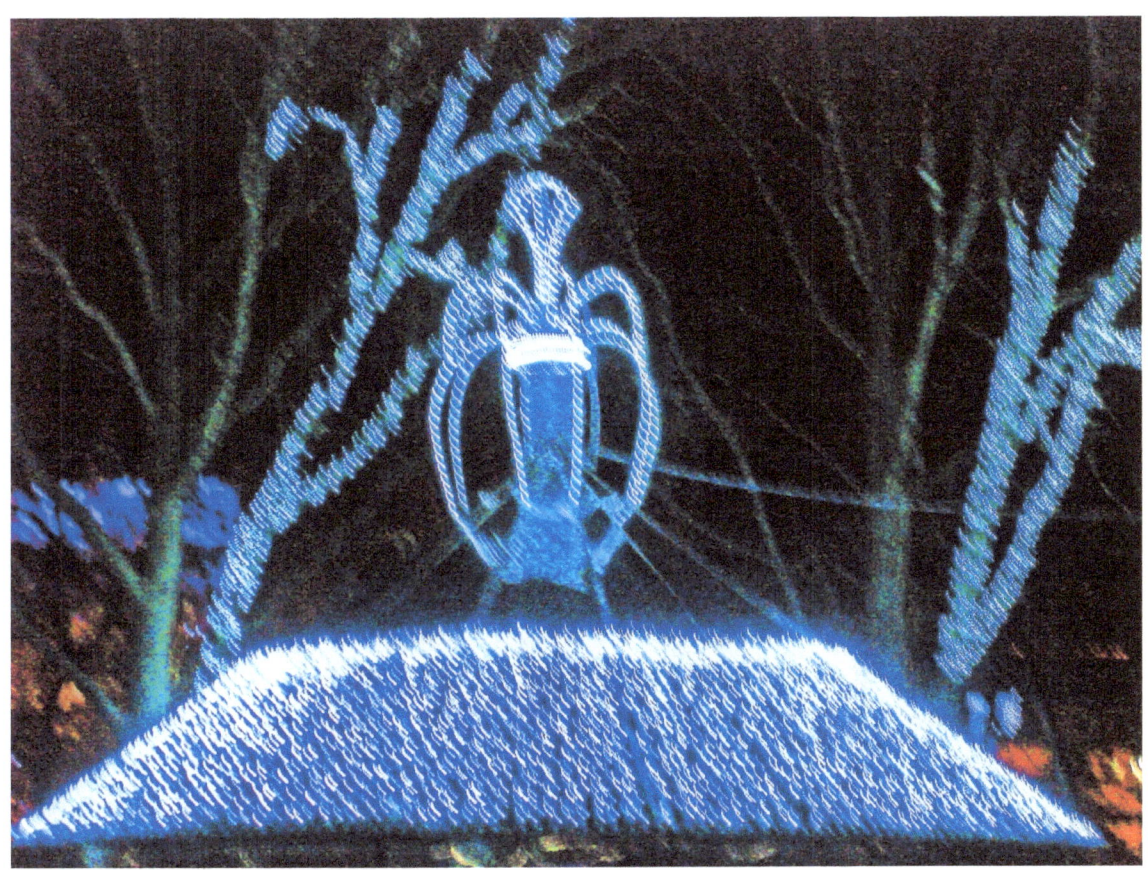

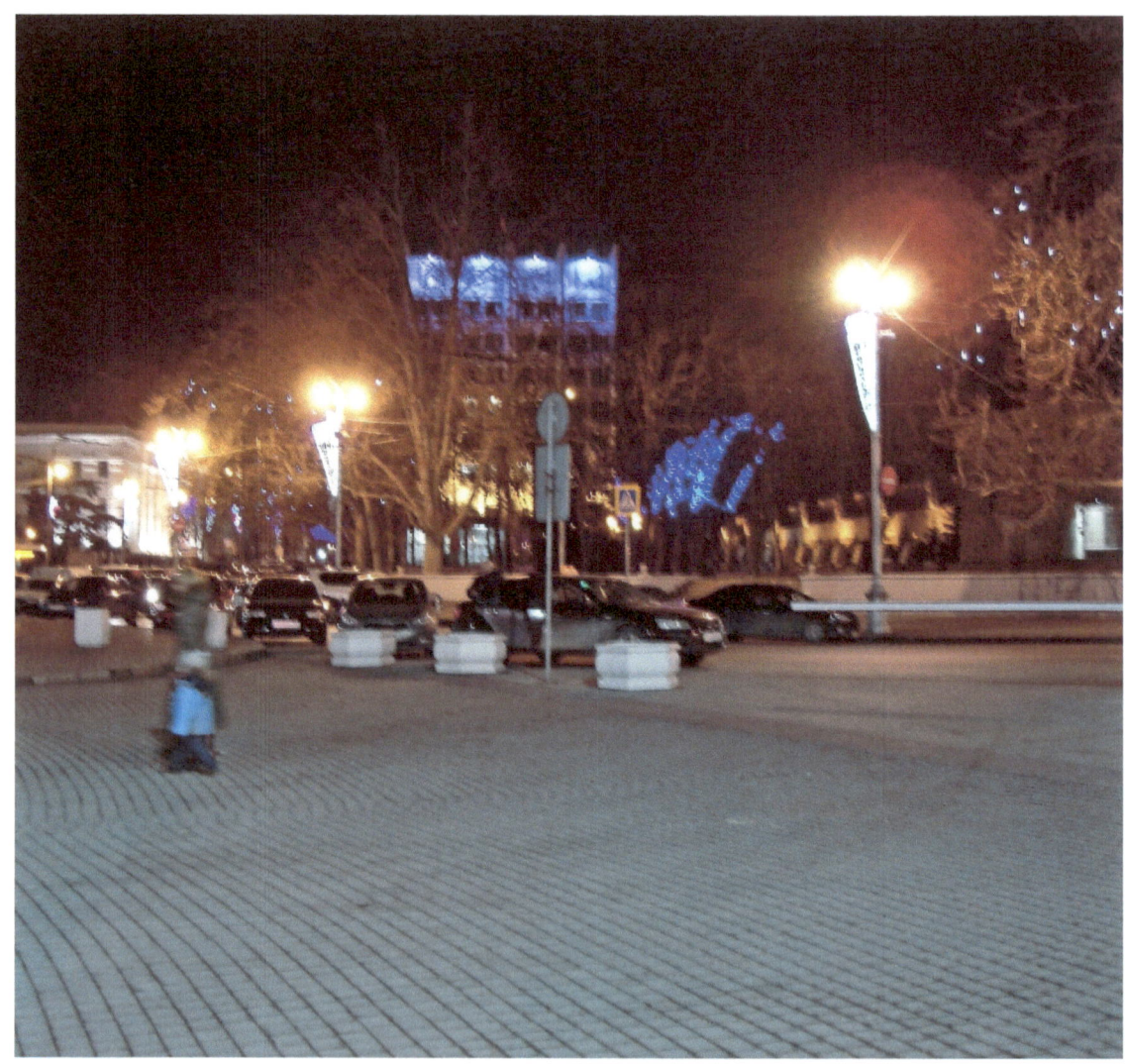

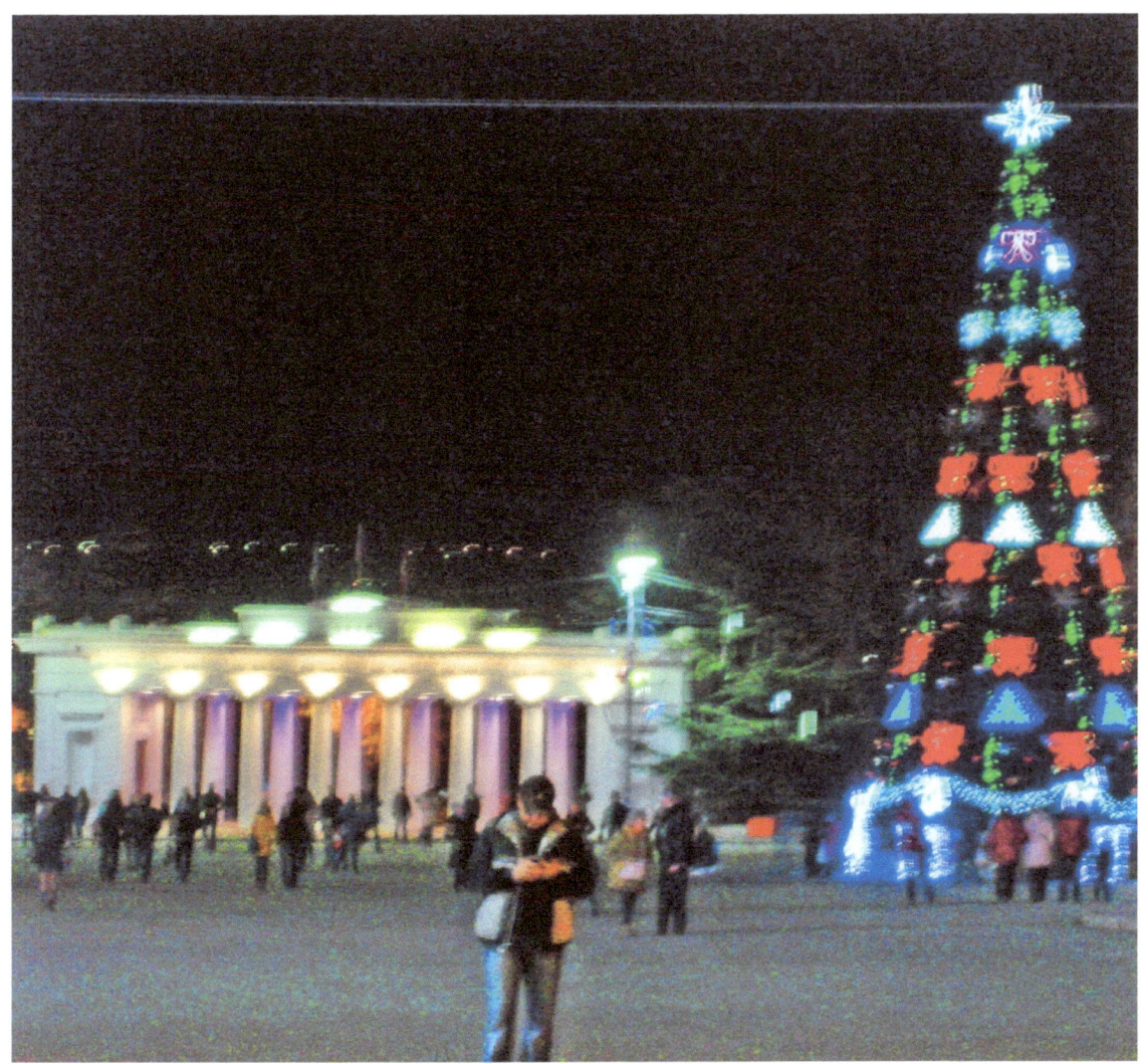

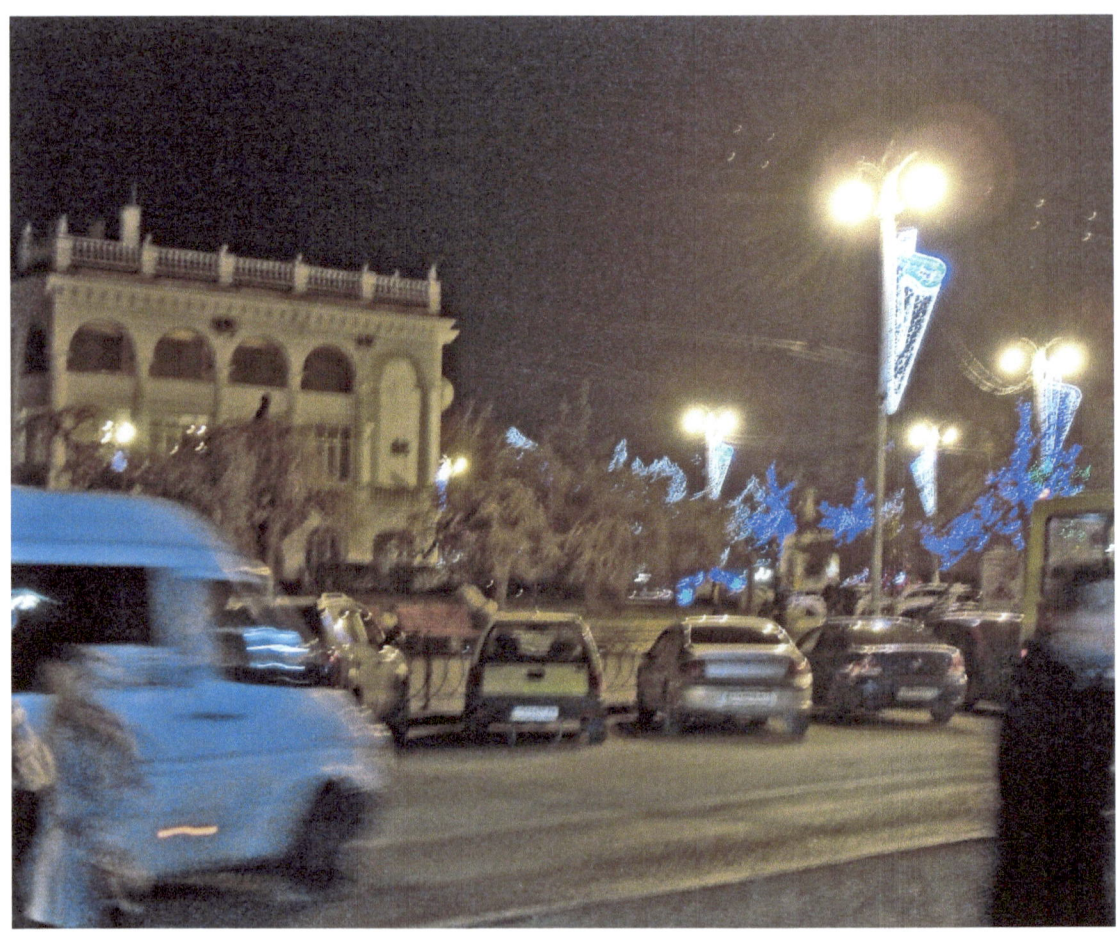

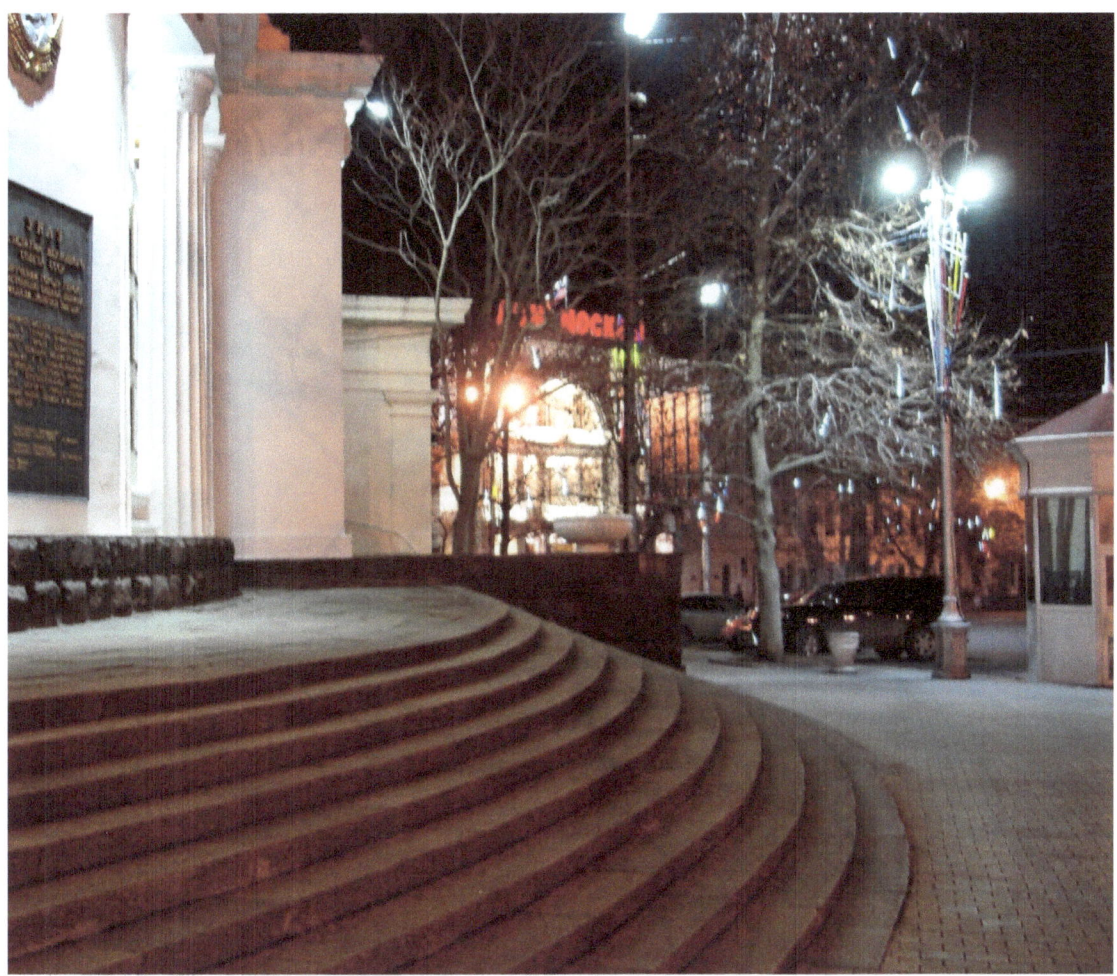

Henry W. Rennengburgton Jr.

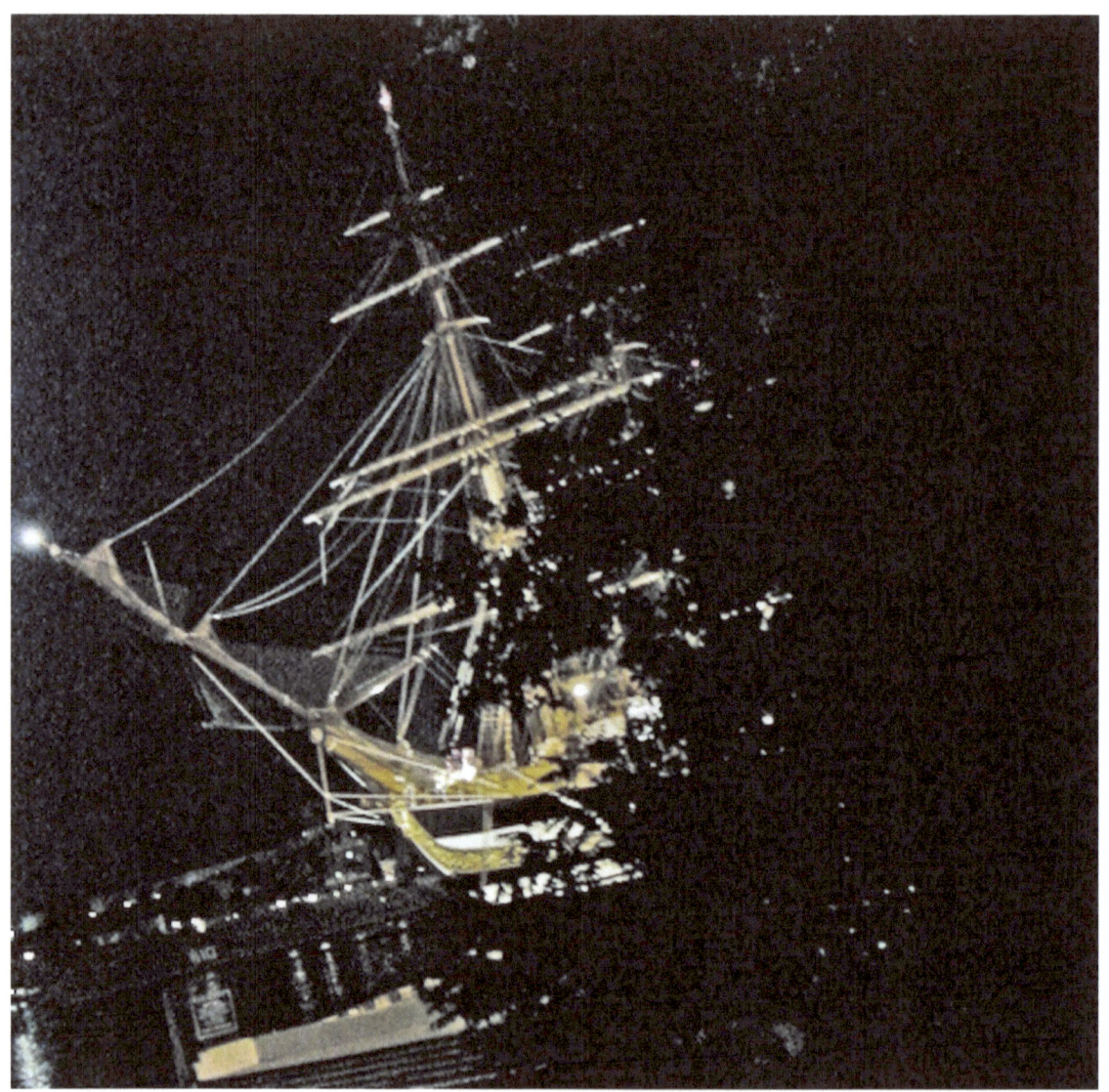

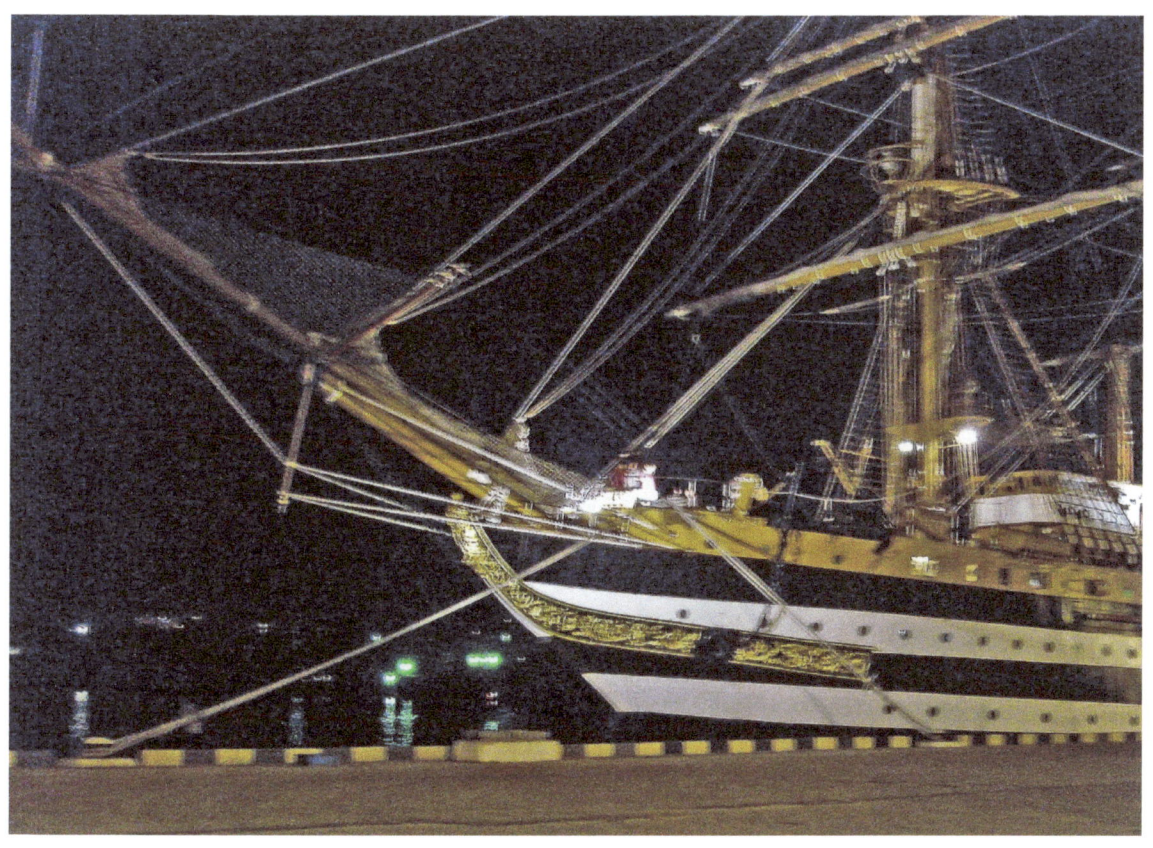

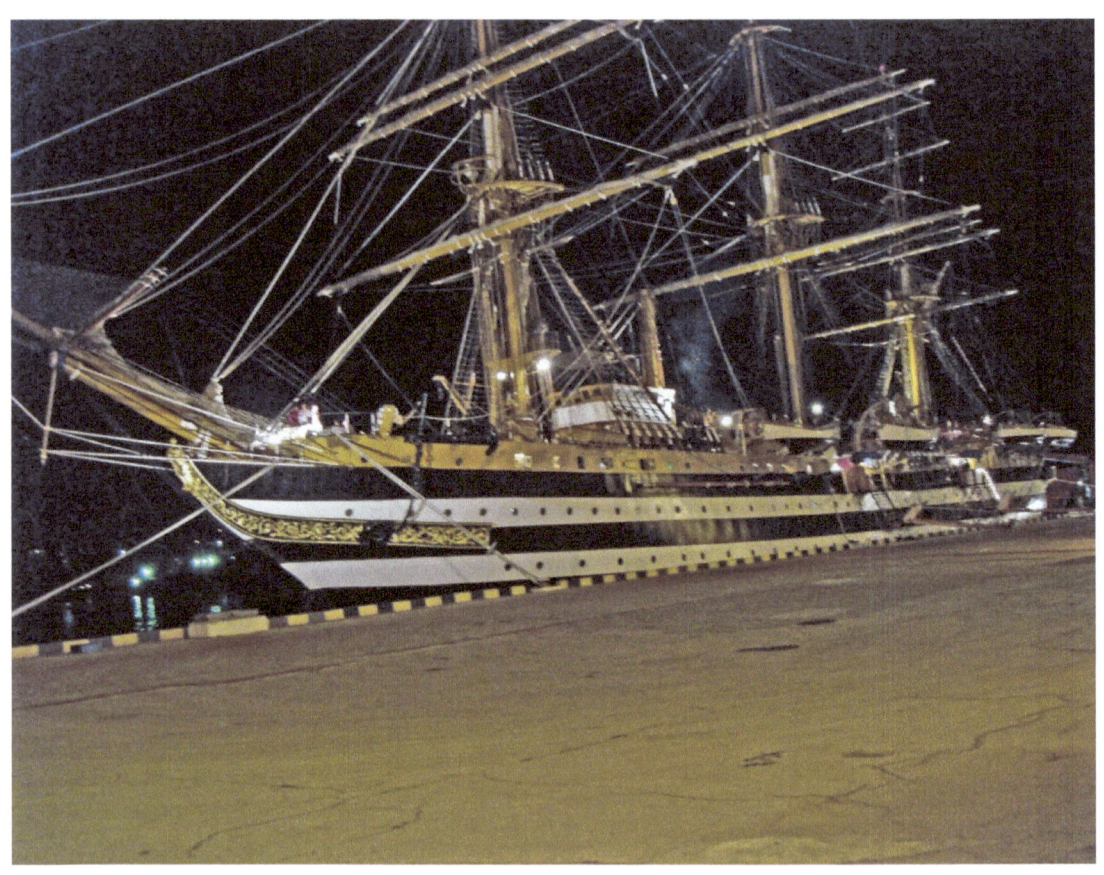

After I took the pictures I see from the sky the beautiful snowflake, very beautiful snowflakes are flying.

Snowflakes floating in the air.
Think of a snowflake, which has a beautiful six symmetric parties.
And this is the perfection of harmony is the source of endless fascination.

The snowflakes were tiny and transparent.
The white world will be soon ... the white sky and the white of the earth.

I see a light snow began to turn in dazzling bright thick dense snowstorm.

ABOUT THE AUTHOR

All photos are the work of author.
23 color photos show the beauty of light decoration of town.
Each photo gives the joy each man who takes the beauty, who is able to receive the beauty who wants to know and to receive the beauty with joy.
Author sees this beauty and gifts this joy to all.